ZOO ANIMALS
IN THE WILD

POLAR BEAR

JINNY JOHNSON

ILLUSTRATED BY GRAHAM ROSEWARNE

W

FRANKLIN WATTS
LONDON•SYDNEY

Ⓐ An Appleseed Editions book

First published in 2006 by Franklin Watts
338 Euston Road, London NW1 3BH

Franklin Watts Australia
Hachette Children's Books
Level 17/207 Kent St, Sydney, NSW 2000

© 2006 Appleseed Editions

Created by Appleseed Editions Ltd,
Well House, Friars Hill, Guestling, East Sussex TN35 4ET

Designed by Helen James
Illustrated by Graham Rosewarne
Edited by Mary-Jane Wilkins

ISBN 0 7496 6727 3

Dewey Classification: 599.786

A CIP catalogue for this book is available from the British Library

Photographs by Getty Images (Theo Allofs, altrendo nature, Wayne R Bilenduke, Tim Boyle,
Daniel J Cox, T Davis / W Bilenduke, Randy Green, Paul Nicklen, Doug Plummer, David Ponton,
Norbert Rosing, Hans Strand, John Warden, Stuart & Michele Westmorland)

Printed and bound in Thailand

Contents

White giants

The polar bear is one of the biggest of all bears. This white giant has a large, powerful body, strong legs, and a short tail. Its head is quite small and it has little furry ears.

A coat of thick fur covers the polar bear's whole body, except for its shiny black nose and the black pads under its feet. Its big furry paws have long curved claws that help the bear grip as it walks on snow and ice. Male polar bears are two or three times bigger than females.

A bear's fur coat has two layers and is up to five cm thick.

4

There are about 400 polar bears living in zoos all over the world. Most of these bears were born and raised in zoos.

A polar bear's huge feet act like paddles in water and snowshoes on the snow.

A big male polar bear can weigh as much as nine grown-up people.

At home in the wild

Polar bears are kings of the ice. They live further north than any other bear. Their home is the Arctic, the area around the North Pole where it is bitterly cold for most of the year.

Polar bears are expert at jumping from one piece of ice to another.

A layer of fat under their fur helps to keep the bears warm. They spend much of their time on the ice sheets that float on the Arctic Sea, but they also live on Arctic islands and coasts. In summer, when much of the sea ice melts, the bears have to find food on land.

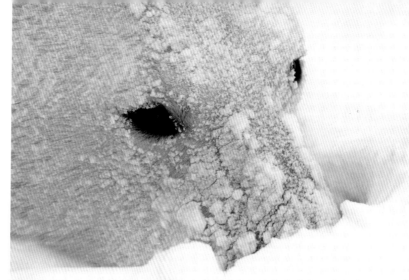

The fur is so thick the bear loses hardly any heat from its body.

In summer, polar bears often hunt on land.

At home in the zoo

Polar bears are used to wandering over a huge area in the wild, so it can be difficult to keep them happy in zoos.

The best zoos give their polar bears enclosures with waterfalls and chilled pools to splash in.

A window next to this enclosure allows zoo visitors to watch the polar bear swim.

All zoos that keep polar bears are now giving them bigger and better enclosures so they don't get bored. Some zoos also provide snow and big blocks of ice to make the bears feel at home.

Zoo bears need plenty to do if they are to stay healthy and contented.

On the move

Polar bears walk for miles over snow and ice as they hunt for food. They can run very fast, but only for short distances.

Unlike most bears, polar bears are good swimmers. Their feet are partly webbed. They have skin between their toes, making their feet into paddles. Under water, a polar bear flattens its ears against the sides of its head and closes its nostrils so water doesn't get into them.

A polar bear swims by pushing itself along with its big front paws, doggy paddle-style.

When a polar bear
comes out of the sea
it shakes the water
out of its fur like a dog.

Waterproof fur helps to protect
the bear from the icy cold water.

Polar bears dive when
hunting prey and can
stay underwater for
up to two minutes.

A polar bear's day

A polar bear has to spend a lot of time looking for food. Only about one in 20 hunts is successful. A polar bear also sleeps for seven or eight hours day, sometimes more in spring and summer.

Polar bears do not hibernate, but mothers with cubs spend several months in a den keeping their young safe and warm. They sleep for much of that time.

Polar bears can sniff out seal pups in their dens beneath the snow.

Polar bears like to keep their white fur clean and may spend 10 to 15 minutes grooming after a meal. They rub water over themselves or rub their fur in the snow to clean it.

Polar bears like to take a nap after a meal. They usually just lie down on the snow, but on very cold days they may dig a hole for shelter.

Rolling in the snow helps a polar bear stay clean.

Zoo bears don't have to hunt for their food. To keep them busy, keepers hide some food in the enclosure for the bears to find.

Feeding time

Polar bears are carnivores, which means they eat meat. In fact they are the largest meat-eating land animals. They have big sharp teeth for attacking their prey.

A polar bear's jaws are lined with 42 strong teeth. It uses these to tear its food apart.

Zoo bears eat fish, meat and some dried food every day. They are also given some lard, cod liver oil and fruit and vegetable treats, such as apples, grapes and carrots.

Seals are the favourite prey of polar bears, but they also eat fish, birds, hares and reindeer. In summer, some polar bears eat leaves and berries too. The bears have a very good sense of smell and can track down seals under the ice by their scent. They can eat huge amounts at one time and then go for weeks without food.

Hunting for food

Polar bears hunt in several different ways. Often, a bear just waits patiently by a hole in the ice. When an unwary seal pops up to take a breath, the polar bear seizes it in its powerful jaws.

Polar bears also stalk their prey. If a bear spots a seal or other animal lying on the ice it creeps up to it. The bear's white fur helps it to stay hidden. When it is as near as it can get without being seen, it makes a high-speed dash to catch its prey.

This bear has spotted a seal in the water and is waiting for it to surface.

A bear gets as close as it can to its prey before making the final pounce.

Polar bears have another way of hunting in spring. This is when ringed seals give birth to their pups in dens under the snow. The bears can sniff these out.

When a bear thinks it has found a pup, it stands up on its back legs and crashes down hard to break into the den with its front legs.

A polar bear is so strong it can break through layers of snow to reach a seal den.

Family life

Polar bears usually live alone, except for mothers rearing cubs. In the months before her cubs are born a mother bear needs to eat plenty of food. Once her cubs are born she will stay with them night and day and will not feed for months.

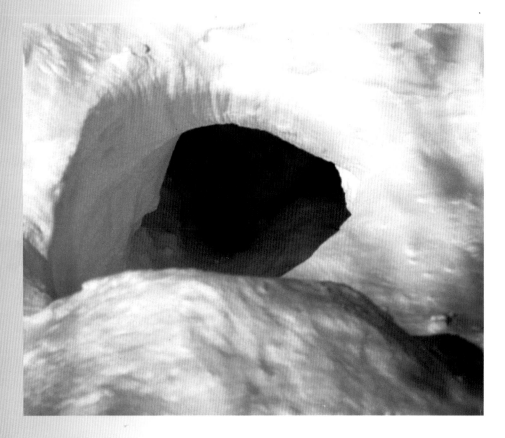

To prepare for her cubs the mother bear digs a den in snow. This usually has a long entrance tunnel leading to one or two areas where the bear and her cubs live.

A polar bear peeks out of her cosy den.

A zoo bear has a special indoor den where she can look after her cubs in peace. She doesn't bring them out until they are three or four months old.

The mother bear gives birth to her babies in this den, which is much warmer than the outside world. She may have up to four cubs, but twins or single cubs are more usual.

A mother bear puts on lots of weight before giving birth.

Baby bears

Baby polar bears are tiny compared with their mum – not much bigger than a rat. They are blind and helpless and spend their first days snuggled close to their mother for warmth.

The cubs spend most of their time feeding on their mother's milk. The milk is very rich and fatty so the cubs grow fast. After about four weeks their eyes are open.

Cubs go on feeding on their mother's milk for two years or more.

Mother bears in zoos usually rear their cubs themselves. But polar bear cubs abandoned by their mothers have been hand reared by keepers. At first the cubs need to be bottle-fed every two hours, day and night.

At two months old the cubs are walking around inside the den, although they are still very wobbly.

Cubs need to practise walking in their den before going out on the slippery snow and ice.

Growing up

In spring, when the babies are a few months old, they peek out of their warm den for the first time. By now they weigh 20 times more than when they were born and are very lively.

Polar bear cubs stay with their mother for at least two years.

A mother polar bear looks after her cubs alone, with no help from the cubs' father.

When a mother bear and her cubs first leave the den she is eager to find food. She has not eaten for a long time and needs to keep up her strength so she can feed her cubs. The cubs begin to eat some meat when they are three or four months old, but they still need their mother's milk, too. Soon they must start learning how to hunt and survive by themselves.

Wild bears rarely live more than 20 years, but zoo bears have been known to live as long as 40.

Playtime

Polar bear cubs learn through play, like all young mammals. When they are strong enough, the cubs love to chase and pounce on one another and they play with mum too. Play builds their muscles and makes them strong.

Adult male polar bears fight seriously when they are competing for mates in spring. They also have play fights.

A mother bear stays very close to her cubs and gives them lots of attention.

Zoo cubs need to play too. The keepers give them lots of toys, such as balls and things they can chew, as well as a paddling pool to splash in.

The bears stand up on their hind legs and wrestle and punch each other without doing any harm. No one knows exactly why they do this, but play fights may help the bears to practise their fighting skills.

These two male polar bears are getting ready for a fight and will try to knock each other off balance.

Keeping in touch

Most polar bears, except mothers with cubs, live alone, but they still need ways of 'talking' to each other when they meet.

A mother talks to her cub with a gentle chuffing sound.

A bear makes a deep growling noise to warn off other bears or to defend its meal. An angry bear may also roar, hiss or snort at enemies.

A mother bear may growl softly at her cubs or cuff them gently with her paw if she needs to scold. She is always ready to defend her cubs fiercely against any enemy, including much larger male polar bears.

This polar bear's lowered head and flattened ears show she is getting ready to charge an enemy.

Polar bear fact file

Here is some more information about polar bears.
Your mum or dad might like to read this, or
you could read these pages together.

A polar bear is a mammal and a member of the bear family.
It is one of the biggest bears, as well as one of the biggest land-
living carnivores – a carnivore is an animal that eats other animals.
Although the polar bear is a land creature, it spends a lot of time in
water. Its scientific name is *Ursus maritimus*, which means sea bear.

Where polar bears live

Polar bears live in the far north in the area around the North Pole. They
spend much of the year on areas of floating ice on the Arctic Sea, but some
polar bears also live in northern Canada, Greenland, Norway and Russia.

Polar bear numbers

There are at least 20,000 polar bears living in the wild and possibly as
many as 40,000. But experts are worried that as the world is getting
warmer, large areas of ice in the Arctic are melting. This will make it
harder and harder for the bears to hunt and their numbers will fall.
The bears depend on being able to move around on the ice in order
to hunt seals, their main food. If too much of the ice melts it will be
difficult for the bears to reach the seals.

Size

A full-grown polar bear is between 2 and 2.5 metres long, with a tail of about 7.5-12 centimetres. It stands about 1.6 metres high at the shoulder. Males weigh between 400 and 600 kilograms, sometimes up to 800 kilograms. Females weigh between 200 and 300 kilograms.

Find out more

If you want to know more about polar bears, check out these websites.

National Wildlife Federation
http://www.nwf.org/wildlife/polarbear/

World Wildlife Fund
http://www.worldwildlife.org/polarbears/index.cfm

Polar Bears International
http://www.polarbearsinternational.org/

Sea World
http://www.seaworld.org/animal-info/info-books/
polar-bear/index.htm

Hinterland Who's Who
http://www.hww.ca/hww2.asp?id=99&cid=8

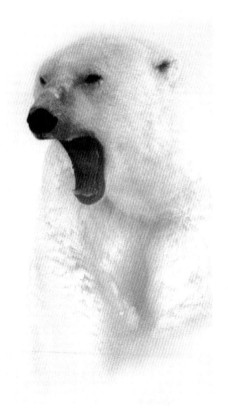

Words to remember

carnivore
An animal that kills
and eats other animals.

den
An animal's home, often
underground. A polar
bear usually digs its
den in a snowdrift.

enclosure
The area where an animal lives in a zoo.

grooming
Cleaning fur to remove dirt, dust and insects.

hibernate
To sleep through the winter months. When an animal
hibernates its temperature falls and its heart rate slows
down, so it uses as little energy as possible.

mammal

A warm-blooded animal, usually with four legs and some hair on its body. Female mammals feed their babies with milk from their own bodies.

North Pole

The furthest north point on Earth.

prey

An animal that is hunted and eaten by another animal.

stalk

To follow something, such as prey, very quietly and carefully

territory

The area where an animal spends most of its time and finds its food.

Index